Osiris Saluki, the magical dog

Fanny Mouchet

Published by Louis Mouchet, 2023.

OSIRIS SALUKI, THE MAGICAL DOG

First edition. May 10, 2023.

ISBN: 979-8223422587

Written by Fanny Mouchet.

Table of Contents

1. OSIRIS

My name is Osiris. What a strange name for a dog, isn't it, my friends?

I come from the oldest canine family, the Salukis. Egypt is my homeland. I am endowed with elegance and lightness. I have muscular legs, a black nose, and strong white teeth. Under black-rimmed eyelids sparkle my almond-shaped eyes. My eyes are soft. My very long ears and tail play an important role in my life. I will explain this to you later.

And what a robe the gods have given me: silky and sand-coloured! When I was born, my grandmother Isis blew three times on my forehead. Her breath circulated all over my body. Thanks to this spell, I acquired the ability to fly and to speak, gifts that only manifest themselves from sunset to sunrise. Yes, my friends, I can fly and speak!

My mother looked at me from a camel-skin collar encrusted with precious stones that, when night comes, shine and throw fires as violent and blinding as headlights. My name is engraved on it in hieroglyphics. It never leaves me.

From the first day of my life, I learned to run and hunt gazelle. My stride is fast and silent. What speed! Seventy kilometers per hour!

When I became an adult, my father appointed me guardian of the Pharaoh Montankhatou, whose mummy was in the Pyrenos pyramid. It was the most beautiful mummy in Egypt. It was a hundred and fifty meters wide. Its top was carved into a point, the façade carved and painted. The entrance was defended by numerous guards. The interior consisted of several rooms. A gallery of difficult access led us to a room decorated with frescoes representing the events of the daily life of the Pharaoh. Four terracotta urns were placed on the floor: the largest contained the monarch's intestines; the oval-shaped one contained his lungs, the longest his stomach, and the smallest his liver. In an adjoining room there were golden chests full of jewels and amulets. In the burial chamber was the sarcophagus with the mummy of the Pharaoh. Artists had painted figures, animals, flowers and various signs on the shrine.

In the offering room, one could admire a pink marble table on which ambrosia had been placed in gilded dishes. Pharaoh's slaves had placed dried figs, hazelnuts, almonds, pistachios, pine nuts, chili peppers, green and black olives, sunflower and sesame seeds in opaline bowls. There was also plenty of wheat and sorghum. Amphorae filled with mead rested at the foot of the sarcophagus.

The Pharaoh's throne was made of wood veneered with gold leaf and the seats carved in precious wood. The skeleton of one of my ancestors rested in a wooden urn decorated with two *salukis*.

This room was also dotted with a variety of objects, such as feather fans, parade daggers with chiseled ivory handles and chests containing shimmering fabrics. Vases were filled with eucalyptus, rose and jasmine.

Everything had to be ready for the living god's long journey to the afterlife. I can't describe all the halls and their riches, there are too many of them. I was proud. It was a great honor to be the guardian of the Pharaoh Montankhatou. I had a very particular work schedule. I would report to my post as soon as the sun shone on the horizon. My brother Horus took over as soon as the moon appeared. When night came, I soared into the sky and flew over all the great capitals of the world.

What a good life for a dog! But, alas, one day it all came to an end.

We were in the middle of a heat wave. I was watching over Montankhatou's sleep when suddenly I heard a dreadful noise. I stood up sharply on my paws. The ground was shaking, the pyramid was rocking from left to right, and then everything turned black. I lost consciousness. When I came to, I opened one eye and then the other. What a sorry sight! The pyramid had collapsed and my brother Horus was crushed under the rubble. Everything was destroyed.

I was wandering among the ruins. I was very lonely. I was groaning, when my eyes were drawn to a glowing, smoking, burning mass. It was a pile of scrap metal burning. Yet I could see a huge, shiny slab. I recognized the wing of one of its birds that noisily roamed the sky and that men call "airplanes". I realized that the metal bird had smashed against the pyramid and that the pyramid had not resisted the shock. Suddenly I saw a goddess lying near the wing, dressed in navy blue, with a gold-brimmed cap and white leather boots. Blonde curls framed her thin face.

She was so beautiful! I approached timidly and licked the palm of my hand. I jumped and stopped, for I saw her eyelashes quiver. I held my breath, then I gently put my head on her breast and I heard: knock, knock, knock, knock, knock...

It was the heartbeat of the goddess. I understood that she was alive. I quickly licked her cheeks. The skin turned pink. She lifted her eyelids slightly, opened frightened blue eyes, looked at me and said:

- Where am I? Where am I? What's happened? What's happened?

The sun was at its zenith and no words could come out of my mouth. I barked, for the flames coming from the wreckage were approaching us. She understood and ran to take refuge under a sycamore tree. I followed her, tears were streaming down her face; she caressed me and said:

- You are my savior. My name is Marianne and what is your name?

I barked three times, which meant in my dog language: O-si-ris.

The sound of this terrible collision resonated throughout the Nile Valley. Bedouins who were camping and napping in an oasis a few leagues away from the disaster were suddenly awakened. The camels blathered. The men thought it was the Thunder God who was getting angry. They looked up to the sky and saw no god. Worried, they scanned the desert and saw a black spot that grew bigger and bigger for life. Stumbling in their jellaba, they went in the direction from which the black smoke was rising. They approached and found nothing but desolation. Then, seeing that the pyramid had been destroyed, they threw it to the ground, moaning:

- Allah, Allah!

When they saw Marianne, they lifted her gently and put her on sheepskins. One of them, taking hold of a gargoyle, poured a drink into her mouth. Another covered her head with flippers to protect her from the sun; a third placed her on the back of a donkey. Then they set off in the direction of Cairo. I followed them, the walk was hard.

I was panting because I was hot and thirsty, the sun was beating down hard. At last, we entered the capital, and as soon as we went to the magistrates of the city, the Bedouins told them what they had seen. We were taken to an air-conditioned office. It was so cool! Marianne was comforted and I was offered a bowl of water. Then the magistrates questioned her. What had happened? Was the pilot ill? Had he fallen asleep? Was there a technical malfunction? Allah knew it.

Marianne drew me close to her and declared:

- I want to go back to my country and take my savior with me.

I was happy; she didn't abandon me. I stayed with Marianne in a big hotel. Everything was very complicated then. I was photographed, and an Egyptologist deciphered the name engraved on my necklace: Osiris Saluki.

And after two days of waiting, I was given a passport on which my name was written in letters illegible to me. I held it to my chest with my right paw. We were taken to the airport and then I got on a plane with Marianne, which had a wing decorated with a white cross on a red background. We flew over the Mediterranean, France, Mont-Blanc and landed in Switzerland at Geneva airport.

2. RINO

My name is Rino. I come from a country where the sun shines and oranges hang from the trees... It's Sicily. That's right, my friends, I'm a little Sicilian and I speak Italian.

I lived at my grandmother's house with my parents and my little brother Pietro. Our house, painted with lime, was very small, and because of lack of space, I slept in the same bed as my grandmother. I called her Nonna. Old, toothless and curved, she always wore a black skirt and bodice. A scarf, also black, covered her white hair. She was the one who prepared the meals and in the evening, she hummed Sicilian songs in a sour voice or told me about the adventures of Giuliano, the outlaw who hid in the mountains. She would describe to me the disasters caused by the volcano that spits fire.

My father worked in the country for a rich landowner. With a scythe on his shoulder, he'd leave early in the morning for his hard work. My mother planted, watered and harvested vegetables for a small garden. I kept our two goats in a nearby field. When night fell, I would take them back to the barn and my grandmother would milk them; I drank good, creamy milk. What a treat!

Life was hard. After careful consideration, my father and mother decided to emigrate to Switzerland. Ah! Switzerland! Land of plenty! What a dream! I saw rivers of frothy milk, chocolate mountains, toys hanging from every tree...

The day of departure arrived. Together with my father, mother and Pietro we left my grandmother and told her:

You'll see, we'll come back rich, very rich, with a big red car, and we'll build a big white marble house with a swimming pool.

She smiled with a nod and greeted us with a trembling hand.

It was a long journey to Switzerland. Now we live on the ground floor of a building in Geneva. There's a bedroom and even a bathroom.

The first time I took a bath, I was afraid of drowning and my mother laughed. This doesn't happen to her very often, because she's very tired. She is a caretaker and gets up at six o'clock in the morning to take the garbage out into the street. During the day, she does housework at private homes. She often goes to the home of a nice lady, Madame Beausoleil, a stewardess who travels around the world. I sometimes meet her on the stairs and she gives me leaflets with beautiful pictures. My father exchanged his scythe for a trowel and became a mason. I have to go to school. Just think, I sit on a chair all day long and I learn a language other than my own, French. How difficult it is! I no longer say "Si, *Signora*", but "Oui, Madame". The teacher calls me all day long.

- Rino, pay more attention!

She keeps staring at me all the time. I dream of my goats, of my Nonna. Nobody understands me. In rage, I gnaw my pencil.

- Rino, put down your pencil!

- Rino, repeat that sentence!

- Rino, write better!

- Rino, Rino, Rino! I've had enough, I don't like school!

And then, one day, everything changes.

It's Sunday, my mom and dad are resting. Sitting on the kitchen floor, my little brother Pietro is playing with the blocks. I'm terribly bored. I take a flyer and cut out the pictures. Suddenly I hear the sound of a car stopping in front of the building. I run to the window and, curious, I look out. It's a taxi. The driver gets out of the car and opens the back door. What do I see? Marianne Beausoleil with a dog! I am still amazed! She pays the driver, takes his suitcase with its colorful stickers from all over the world and enters our building followed by the dog. Intrigued, I run into the hallway and stick my eye through the peephole. No, I'm not dreaming, it's Marianne. She enters the elevator with the dog and disappears on the way up. I go back to my room. A great sadness overcomes me. I give up my cut-out and think: Oh, if I had a dog! My loneliness would be less. I lie down on my bed and close my eyes. I fall asleep and dream of colorful dogs waving friendly at me.

Days go by. From my window, I watch Marianne and her dog. She walks him on a braided leather leash. He has a strange collar around his neck decorated with strange drawings. She must be on holiday, because I often see her on the way up the building and in the street. This morning, on my way to school, I ventured to pet the dog; he put his paw on my hand and looked at me for a long time.

It's feeding time. My mother puts a large platter of spaghetti with rosemary-scented tomato sauce on the table.

I love spaghetti; I savor it, wrap it around my fork, then drop it in my mouth and skillfully unroll it. Suddenly, the ringing sound resounds. Who can come at this hour. Curious, I put down my fork, rush out and open the door. Marianne is standing on the landing.

- Hello, Rino. Is your mother here?

- Yes, ma'am... Mama! Mama! Mama! Mummy! Mummy! Mummy! You're wanted!

- Hello, Mrs. Beausoleil. Are you on vacation?

- Yes, and I have a favor to ask you, dear Mrs. Salvatore. I'm going back to work tomorrow. I'm going to Mexico and I can't take my dog with me. Could you take him to boarding school? Of course, I will pay you, and I think your son Rino would be happy to take care of him. He's a well-behaved, clean, quiet dog.

I can feel my heart breaking. My gaze does not leave my mother's lips. What will she answer?

Of course, Madame Beausoleil, I am happy to do you this service.

Marianne leaves and comes back with the dog and a big cone full of meat croquettes and dried cod.

- Dear Rino, I entrust you with my dog. His name is Osiris and he's from Egypt. Take good care of him, for he's the apple of my eye.

- Yes, Madame Beausoleil, you can count on me.

With Marianne gone, I go into my room, put a blanket next to my bed and arrange the meat croquettes on a plate.

- Come, Osiris, come close to me, we already know each other! Here, eat!

He barks three times, tilts his head and, with his long teeth, grabs the food. I give him a drink from a bowl. When it's time to go to sleep, I caress him, jump into bed and fly off to dreamland.

The day dawns, a bark wakes me up. It's Osiris and I understand that he means: "Rino, hurry up, you'll be late for school".

What a bad day! Everything goes wrong: I sing wrong, I answer wrong and I stumble at the gym lesson. I can't wait to see Osiris again.

Finally, the day ends. My mother says to me:

- Before going to bed, take Osiris for a while in the square and don't linger!

What a long night! I can't get to sleep. I sit in a suit on the blanket next to Osiris and confide in him:

- Oh! Osiris! I'm in a lot of pain. I'm bored with my Sicily and my grandmother.

- There are other kids more miserable than you.

I'm startled, look around and don't see anyone. I ask out loud:

Who spoke?

- It's me, Osiris.

I'm pinching my thigh: no, I'm not dreaming.

There's no such thing as a talking dog!

- I'm a magic dog: I talk and I fly.

- How can you fly? You have no wings.

- Look, look, look, look! I'll give you a little demonstration. Above all, be quiet and lock your bedroom door. No one must know of my power. Like squirrels, I fly through the air with my tail. This is my rudder. Then I raise my ears horizontally. I sniff once: they turn slowly like propellers. Second sniff: look, I'm going up, I'm going up! I touch the ceiling, I turn around the chandelier! I close and open my eyes three times: they project a strong light. My phosphorescent whiskers blink and guide me like a radar. Man and his mechanics are no match for me. Look out, I'm landing!... As you can see, my flight is silent. Are you convinced?

I was amazed, I was stunned.

- When I lived in Egypt, I flew every night to visit the capitals of the world: Paris, London, Rio de Janeiro... I'm in Geneva by chance. Now listen to me carefully!

- Yes, yes, Osiris, I am all eyes and ears.

- Have you ever visited Geneva?

- No, Osiris. My parents work all day and at night they're tired. I don't go out much.

- Okay. Tonight we've talked enough, but tomorrow, if you apply yourself in class, when the night comes, you'll come with me and we'll discover this city together. Sleep, tomorrow you have to go to school.

- Good night, Osiris. Thanks to you, my dreams will be sunny.

- Good night, Rino! I'll see you in the morning!

3. GENEVA

The next day I sleep all day, and when the moon appears, I snort and look at the alarm clock: it is twenty-two o'clock. I have to wake Rino up, I tell myself. I have to keep my promises, especially with the children. I tickle his feet with my whiskers and pinch his ears.

- Huh!... Huh! Huh! Huh!

- Rino... Rino...

- What's going on? What's going on?

- Get up! Get up! You're about to get your first flight. Take it easy, we're going on a trip.

- Oh, fancy! Where's my shirt?

- There she is... Are you dressed?

- Yes.

- Open the window! Straddle my back and hold on to my collar. Are you ready?

- Yes, Osiris.

- Careful, I'm sniffing: a... ...two... three... I'm taking off, I'm rising, I'm high. Lucky her, no clouds! Visibility is good. It's a full moon. Look at the sky! Look at the clouds! There is the Little Dipper.

- I don't see a bear!

- Rino, your knowledge is meager. You have a lot to learn. Little Dipper is a constellation, a set of stars that form a wagon. At the end of the tiller, the North Star throws rays as bright as a diamond. It points north and is most visible in the month of October. If you can locate the stars correctly, you can guide yourself without using a compass...

- Teach me more star names.

- There is the Eagle, the Swan, the Dolphin, the Winged Horse and many more.

- Say, Osiris, I'm going to become a scientist in your company!

- Let's fly over the bay of Lake Geneva and pass by the water jet. Its power throws the water more than a hundred meters high... Over there, on your right, is the UN.

- Osiris, what does UN mean?

- United Nations. This is where the nations of the world try to resolve their conflicts.

- Does it also exist for dogs?

- No, we don't have all these problems. We obey the laws of nature... Let's take a look at the Rhone River; before it flows into France, it waters the Geneva countryside. Let's jump over the Mont Blanc bridge.

- Why is it called Mont Blanc?

- From this bridge you can see the Mont-Blanc, a mountain with eternal snow, the highest in Europe. Look at its white peak dawning in the distance... Here, Île Rousseau; it's very small. In its garden, the statue of the illustrious writer Jean-Jacques Rousseau sits enthroned. The birds are not very respectful, they use it as a perch.

- Tell me about him.

- His father was a watchmaker, and he gave his son a piece of advice that can be found in school textbooks: "My son, love your country".

- Which country should I like, Switzerland or Italy?

- Love them both!

- Osiris, I am told that Geneva is a welcoming city. Me, I find it cold and the Genevans reserved.

- Perhaps it is the icy kiss that influences the mood of the Genevans. Let's go back.

- It's like playing leapfrog! Oh, a flowery clock!

- It's the biggest one I know. The needles are metal. Colored flowers make up the numbers that stand out on a dial of white flowers. At the beginning of each season, the gardener offers us another harmony of flowers.

- When I have money, I'll buy a postcard with the water jet and another one with the flowered clock. I'll send them to my Nonna. She'll be amazed, she who's never left her village.

- Let's go up to the old town dominated by St. Peter's Cathedral.

- Is the saint made of stone?

- Hi, Hi, Hi! But no, Peter is a biblical character. Listen to the chimes of the cathedral:

Let's go dancing under the elm trees
Bring young girls to life
Oh, come on, now...

- It was Jean-Jacques Rousseau who composed this song, he was a fine musician. The walls that we see protected the city in the past. In the year 1602, the Savoy coveted the city of Geneva. There was a famous battle.

- Tell, tell quickly.

- The Savoyards, armed with sharp spears and carrying long wooden ladders, wanted to seize the city during the night. Blood was spilled, and a brave housewife, Mother Kingdom, capped a Savoyard with a pot full of hot soup. The escalation aborted. Savoyards and Swiss smoked the peace pipe and today they get along wonderfully. Rejoice, every year on the 12th of December, confectioners sell little chocolate pots filled with marzipan vegetables, and children dress up to celebrate this victory.

- Me, I'll disguise myself as a Sicilian shepherd.

- Look at that old pink building, that's Calvin's college. It's named after a character who made quite a splash with a rather complicated religion. One thing I do remember is that Calvin preached austerity. Men were not to wear gold or silver chains, and women were not to wear embroidery or jewelry. They learned to save money. Do you have a piggy bank?

- Yes, I have a little pink piggy.

- Slip in your pocket money and, when it's full, take it to the bank, you'll get rich. Small streams make great rivers.

- I'll take your advice. Whose is that white flag with the red cross flying in the window of this house?

- He belongs to the Red Cross, an association founded by Henri Dunant, an admirable man! White is the symbol of innocence and peace. The Red Cross intervenes during wars, earthquakes, floods, famine or any other disaster.

- My grandmother told me that an earthquake destroyed the city of Messina.

- That's right. So doctors, nurses, and volunteers do something about it. Ambulances and trucks with a red cross carry the wounded, medicine, food, clothes, tents and blankets.

- When my little piggy gets full, I'll give them my money.

- You have a good little heart, Rino. Let's continue our round, here's Place Neuve square with the Grand Theatre and the Conservatory.

- What is canned in it?

- Hi, hi, hi, nothing, they teach music.

- I'd like to play the drum. At the music lesson, Mrs. Merle told me I had good ears.

- If you study well, you will be able to take courses at the Conservatory and the University; there she is in front of us.

- This morning's headline was about the university and Jean Pi... Pi...

- Piaget, he was a biologist who wrote a lot of books. He studied the behavior of albino sparrows and mollusks.

- I don't know what a mollusk is.

- The snail is one of them.

- Oh, is that right? I know a song:

Big Horned Snail

Show me your horns

if you...

- Bravo, you're just singing. But I go on, the oyster is also a mollusk. I fished one once in the Indian Ocean and when I opened it, what a surprise! It contained a pearl as big as a pigeon's egg; it was worth a fortune. Alas, I had hidden it in the pyramid behind the Pharaoh's ear. It disappeared in the disaster. Let's forget about it and return to our eminent Piaget. He has also studied the development of intelligence in children.

- Am I smart, Osiris?

- Your pertinent questions prove you're a smart kid.

- I wonder if there are biologists in dogs, too.

- At the moment, we have no research scientists. We rely on our instincts... Oh, oh, oh, oh! We're approaching the airport. Let's avoid it, I don't want to be spotted by the control tower.

- Osiris, the wind is rising.

- Yes, the water jet changes direction. It's a sign of rain, let's go home quickly. Let's go along the street, avoid the chimneys, turn left... Careful, I'm starting the descent. Tighten your legs against my sides. One... two... three... five... seven... here's our building! Let's go in through the window, keep your head down... Whack: successful landing! Get undressed and go to sleep quickly. Tomorrow, you have to be fresh for your school day.

- Yes. Yes, I remember the song: *Let's go to sleep under the elm trees...*

That's not quite right, but he fell asleep. Now it's my turn to fall into the arms of Morpheus.

4. PARIS

We went a week without traveling.

During the night from Monday to Tuesday, we do not fly.

On Tuesday mornings, Rino's teacher has a predilection for written questions.

It's Wednesday, daylight is gradually fading away. Waiting for Rino, I dream of our next trip. He should have left school more than an hour ago. The loneliness is starting to weigh on me. I feel the need to stretch not only my legs, but also my ears and tail. Finally, my friend arrives in a pitiful state with a poached eye, torn clothes and a face smeared with tears.

- By Allah, Rino, what is the matter with thee?

- Sniff... Sniff... I got into a fight with Paul, the son of the local grocer. He told me I was a dirty macaroni and that I spoke French with a stutter. He tripped me, I punched him in the nose and the fight went on. All the students blamed me and the supervisor kept me in class for an hour. Sniff. Sniff... However, I didn't start it. My mother will be summoned and I'll be punished. Oh! Why didn't I stay in Sicily? I had good friends there. Sniff... Sniff.

- Come on, dry your tears Rino, it's okay. You'll explain everything to your parents, they'll understand.

- Yes, but my clothes are torn... We don't have much money.

- Listen, take your bath and put on your pajamas like you do every night. Hurry up, because your mother's coming home from work. Tonight, we're leaving for Paris.

- When the family was at the table, Rino commented on the argument. His parents were understanding because they sometimes suffered from the cold attitude of the Genevans.

The father consoled his son; he was proud of his bravery.

- When I was your age, I fought every day!

- Rino's mother replied:

- Yeah, but this is different. The clothes are nothing, I'll mend them. My son was insulted.

- He must learn to defend himself. In his life, he will see many others!

- Let's eat this nice plate of spaghetti. I can't wait to go to bed. I'm dead tired.

After dinner, we retire to our room. Through the window I see the moon, which is full and seems to wink at me. I wait until the whole family is asleep and call Rino. He jumps on my back, and off he goes. We fly to Paris.

Ten minutes later, we are above the Eiffel Tower, the most visited monument in the world.

- So, Osiris, this is the Eiffel Tower? It looks like a piece of junk!

- That's true, but when you're on top, you dominate the whole city. It has a height of three hundred and twenty metres and is useful for the transmission of radio and television programmes. We will see more interesting and beautiful things. Look at that long avenue: it is the Champs-Elysees, we will go up it.

- Oh Osiris! A star of light!

- This is the Place de l'Étoile, it bears this name because twelve avenues radiate from it like the branches of a star. In the center stands the Arc de Triomphe and under its arcade the flame of the Tomb of the Unknown Soldier shines. Let's continue our visit!

- Stop, Osiris! What's this big church all lit up?

- It's Notre Dame Cathedral. You're a mason's son, you'll be interested. Do you realize that it's over seven hundred years old and took over a hundred years to build? The walls are thick and solid and....

- Yes, yes, look at those grimacing animal statues with gaping maws! They frighten me.

- They're gargoyles, rainwater is ejected through the animals' mouths. This avoids the degradation of the walls.

- Oh, Osiris, houses on a river!

- This is the Seine, and these floating houses are barges. They carry goods. Careful, Rino, don't lean over... eh... Rino... Rino!...

Poof!

- Damn, he fell in the water. I've got to get him out quickly because he can't swim.

- Help, Osiris, help, I'm drowning!

- Hang on, I'm coming; hold on to my collar. Phew! You're saved, but you're all wet.

There's a man approaching us.

- Who goes there? My word, there's a child! What's he doing here at such a late hour? You're soaking wet, my boy, what happened to you?

- Uh... (Clears throat) Uh... I was walking my dog to pee; I leaned over to look at the barges, I slipped and fell into the water. My dog jumped in the river and saved me.

- What a brave dog you have there! You'll catch cold, come on my barge, you'll dry yourself by the stove. Come on board!... Loulette, look who I brought you! The kid fell in the water.

- Hello, little guy! You're shivering, come and warm up! Are you hungry?

- A little, sir.

- Good thing I still have a piece of leek pie, a Picardy specialty. Drink this coffee hot! It's not strong, I put a lot of chicory in it. And you, my dog, eat these biscuits. I'm out of meat.

- Wow, wow.... wow!

- Thank you, ma'am, I'm enjoying your pie. It's delicious. My clothes are dry, we're going to leave you because mummy will be worried. Goodbye, and thank you again.

- You're welcome, my boy. If you come to Picardy, maybe we'll meet again. My name is Lechêne and my barge is the Rose des Vents...

- Phew! Rino, we're safe and sound. Anybody on the dock?

- No. No, no, no, no, no, no, no, no.

- Jump on my back and let's go to the dog cemetery... There he is! Hold on tight, I'm landing.

- What beautiful graves!

- Now that you know the alphabet, decipher the epigraph on that tombstone.

- To my Medor, my trusty friend. There's even his photo. What kind of dog was it?

- A German shepherd.

- I continue: To the eternal memory of your old Tata Michèle... Oh, but I learned her song at school:

It's mother Michèle.

who lost her cat.

- Do we only bury dogs?

- No, all pets are allowed. Of course, since dogs are man's best friend, there are more of them in the house... Let's get closer to this equestrian statue. It guards the tomb of the Shooting Star, a famous racehorse.

- Do you want to be buried here?

- Oh no, I hope to be buried in Egypt, in our family vault... Let's change the decor, let's visit the live animals. Hop, starting position and heading for the Zoo of Vincennes... Let's stop by the lions' enclosure and ask them: Hup, hup! Good evening lions! Can you hear me?

- RRRRRRRRRRRR. . . . rrrrrrrrrrron who's talking? My word, you're a dog, you're strictly forbidden entry, and for you, my boy, visiting hours are long over. Do we have any idea of waking up honest people at such a late hour? Don't you know we bind them; we need seventeen hours of sleep a day? Get out, out, or I'll call the warden!

- Please, Mr. Lion, we have come a long way to investigate the lives of animals in captivity. Don't you miss the freedom. Don't you miss the savannah, the baobabs and the gazelles?

- No, not at all, here I am housed, fed and cared for. What more could I want? If the visitors are noisy, I go in and rest in my cave. I leave the savannah to the other animals. As for the gazelles, it's the lionesses that chase them, we males are too lazy. Ask my wife Bobonne instead. Excuse me if I yawn, I'm sleepy.

- Hello, Mrs. Lioness, are you happy in this zoo?

- It's hard for me to answer you because I was born here. I'm not unhappy. Because I know nothing about Africa. I heard the guards talking about a reservation called Thoiry. My children will never see the savannah. I wish they could live in Thoiry. What I don't wish for is a life of circus, menagerie and cramped cages. Good night, dear visitors, my twins are asking for their feed.

- Goodbye, Madam Lioness, may all your wishes come true.

- And now, let's continue our investigation into our cousins the wolves.

- There they are, Osiris, walking non-stop back and forth. How unhappy they look!

- Whoo-hoo... whoo-hoo! You said it, kid, we're sad and unhappy. Wolves love the steppe and the forests! It's out of boredom that we walk all day long. Believe me, it's better to have a hard life and an empty stomach, but to be free. Visitors slander us and tell their children: "Here is the bad wolf who will eat you if you are not wise! "

- It's true, Monsieur le Loup, my grandmother always told me the story of Little Red Riding Hood.

- It's just a legend, we're peaceful and have a sense of honor. We do not attack man if he lets us live in peace.

- Dear cousin, we must leave you, perhaps we shall meet again someday!

- Ooh... ooh... bye!

- Did you notice the gorilla in his cage? He's shot and he's not moving.

- Yes Osiris, if I'm sad, I don't feel like running, I'm numb and I feel like crying. The gorilla must be very sad.

- Except for the lion, all the animals seem unhappy.

- I've got an idea!

- Which one, Rino?

- Let's free all the animals in the zoo!

- You don't think about it, Rino! In winter, most of these animals go back to their lodgings, they can't resist our climate and wouldn't survive in the wild. They demand special food.

- You're right, I hadn't thought about all those problems. Let's just set the wolves free! They are the ones who suffer most from their captivity.

- Well, fine, let's give them their freedom and, back to Geneva.

Since that day, the howling of the wolves can be heard again in the forests of Europe.

As soon as Rino's head was on the pillow, he dreamed that he was running away with the wolves back to his home village. The next day, a surprise awaited him.

5. THE RETURN OF MARIANNE

- Osirissss!.... Osirissssss!

- What's going on, Rino? You're out of breath.

- I passed Marianne Beausoleil on the way up. I'm scared! I'm scared! What will become of us? Will she take you back? I love you so much, my dear Osiris, I can no longer live without you.

- Wipe your tears and calm down. There's no need to panic. I also prefer your company to that of an adult ... Careful... she's talking to your mother, let's be quiet and open our ears.

- Good evening, Mrs. Salvatore.

- Good evening, Madame Beausoleil, did you have a good trip?

- Oh, yes! Mexico is a wonderful country. Tomorrow I'm going back to Brazil. And how is Osiris doing?

- Very well, dear lady. Just imagine that since your dog is with us, my son is doing better at school. His teacher summoned me. She's pleased with Rino's progress.

- I'm very comfortable with that, and I just wanted to ask you if you wouldn't mind keeping it for a while longer. I asked my manager to ask if I could take my dog along during flight hours. He told me to read the rules and regulations: "No employee may be accompanied by an animal."

- Don't torment yourself, ma'am. My son will be happy to hear the news... Rinooo! Rinooo! Come with Osiris!

- Did you hear that, Rino? We are saved! I'm staying with you, let's rush to her!

- Hello, Madame Beausoleil!

- Hello, little one. Oh, how muscular Osiris is! You take good care of him. Open this package! I brought you a souvenir from Mexico.

- Chic, a leather belt with stones and a drawing!... How beautiful!

- The stones are turquoise and the design an Aztec sundial. The Indians know the time by observing the shadow of the stem which is reflected on the dial. By the way, I'm going back on a trip and I entrust Osiris to you again.

- Thank you, thank you very much, ma'am. It's time for his walk. Follow me, Osiris, let's go to the square.

- Whoa! Whoa!

- Let's get out of here before she changes her mind.

- Tonight we will not leave the room... Sneezy. I have a cold. Next time we won't go to Brazil, I don't want to come face to face with Marianne.

- You're always thinking straight... This morning, Mrs. Merle, my teacher, was astonished. She read us a text about France and asked us a lot of questions. I was the only student who raised his hand. I'm becoming the most knowledgeable in geography.

- Sneezy. Sneezy! Let's go back home. The wind is blowing hard, I'm cold and I'm shaking like a leaf. I'm still not used to Geneva's humid climate. Let's go home, Rino.

- Here's your blanket by the radiator, lie down my poor friend, I'll cover you with my wool sweater, you'll warm up quickly and tomorrow you'll be all right. I'll run to the kitchen to fetch you some warm milk... Here, drink! I've added a spoonful of mountain honey.

- I'm not a bear! I don't like sugary drinks!

- You make me laugh; your voice is all hoarse! Mom always says it's a good remedy for the throat. Drink quickly before the milk gets cold.

- Thank you, Rino, and good night.

- Good night, Osiris. I'm so happy you're not leaving me!

- No, Rino, not for now, but when you grow up one night I'll fly back to my country.

6. NEW YORK

Lying on the bedside table with my head between my legs, I'm thinking. Rino sleeps peacefully. Where could we go tonight? Suddenly I have an idea.

- Rino... Rino... Wake up! Wake up! Wake up! Tell me, what day is it?
- Well... well... I think October 31st.
- That's what I thought. Have you heard of Halloween?
- Hello... hello... what?
- Halloween is the day before All Saints' Day and a holiday for all little Americans. They dress up and beg for treats from everyone in their neighborhood... Beware of those who don't give them anything! The next day, they find rubbish on their mats or their windows smeared with soap. Do you feel like going to New York?
- Oh, yes! Fancy! I'll bring back some candy.

As soon as said, as soon as done, with Rino on my back, I take the direction of America, cross the Atlantic Ocean and go along the east coast of the United States.

Rino is surprised to see that it is still daylight. I forgot the six-hour time difference between Geneva and New York.

- What time is it, Osiris? The sun is still shining.
- It's four o'clock in the afternoon.
- So we can't land?
- No, of course, I'm flying low, above the clouds. No one can spot us. Let's execute a reconnaissance tour over the city. Take my magic glasses from under my collar. You can see everything.
- Thank you, Osiris, have you ever been to New York?
- Yes, with Grandma Isis.
- I remember it well. What bothers me is that I don't know whether to turn left or right to get over the island.
- An island?
- Yes, New York City is built on an island.

- Then it's very small.

- No, it's big, it's one of the most populous cities in the world... Oh, oh, oh, oh! A wind-haired witch riding a broom is coming up on our left. She's just in time, we'll ask her for directions... Good evening, Madam, can you give us some information?

- Good evening, my little ones. Speak up. I have a hard ear because I'm 300 years old. I'm getting old!

- Directions to New York City, please, ma'am.

- Ah well, I know it very well, for two hundred and fifty years I've been making the trip every year. I take advantage of the Halloween party to visit my cousins in America. You turn left by the bat-shaped cloud, then right by the hippopotamus-shaped cloud. You can't go wrong! At the entrance to the harbor, you'll see the Statue of Liberty.

- Thank you very much ma'am and have a good trip.

- Hold on to my collar, I'm going to make a left turn; a right turn and a left turn.

- I see a colossal statue holding a torch, is it the Statue of Liberty?

- Yes, with Grandma Isis we went up into her head and beyond, we admired the whole city. The sea air gave it a verdigris patina. The houses that climb to the sky are skyscrapers.

- What's the name of the one who dominates everyone else?

- The Empire State Building, it's 102 stories high...

As a light mist covers the city, I land on the outside gallery. We'll rest, I have to stretch my limbs... One... two... three... successful!

- Why are there so many phone booths behind that glass door?

- These are not telephone booths but small studios where tourists can record their voices. After their visit, they take home a souvenir from New York. Would you like to try these devices?

- Yes, but we don't have any money!

- Grandma Isis collected coins from all over the world. I have a few dollars under my collar. Take one!

And the two buddies recorded "Little Santa Claus".

- What do we do now? The sea air whets my appetite.

- Let's look for a snack bar, because in America, dogs are not allowed in restaurants.

- What's a snack bar?

- A snack bar is a small café where you can get your fill of quickly cooked food. Snack means: on the go; it is appreciated by people in a hurry. This one seems welcoming, push the door open and let's sit on these stools! We will be served faster. I don't dare to order; the waitress would be surprised to hear a talking dog. Press three times on the red stone of my collar, you'll get simultaneous translation. The waitress will understand you even if you mispronounce, she's used to serving foreign tourists.

- One, two, three... please ma'am, I want two servings of pancakes drizzled with maple syrup and two ice milks.

- What flavor, kid?

- Chocolate... Thank you, ma'am.

- Mmm! What a delight! And what big portions! Six pancakes piled on top of each other! I won't be hungry for candy anymore.

- Eat fast! I can see through the window a mounted policeman with his eyes fixed on us. If he came in and asked us for our papers, we'd be borrowed. It's better to keep him out of our company.

- I wipe my mouth and I'm ready.

- Let's take a walk, cross that bridge that leads us into the old part of Brooklyn and join this group of children near the church.

- They are in disguise, Osiris, and I am not.

- That's right, let's think about it.... Do you see that sheet on the rack? Let's grab it and wrap yourself up like a ghost.

- That's stealing!

- No, the tenants of this house are absent, the shutters are closed. We'll put it back... What a beautiful ghost! Listen to the password: "Treat... *or... Trick*".

- Faster! Faster! Faster!

- *Treat* or *Trick*!

- All right... let's get closer to that little redheaded guy in the cat mask. He's so funny.

- Hi, there.

- Hi, you have a beautiful dog, what's your name?

- Rino, and my dog, Osiris.

- I'm Mike, I haven't seen you around.

- No, we're just passing through.

- Come with me and let's start with the red brick house.

- I'll knock on the door first.

- Knock... knock... knock... knock... "Treat or Trick"

- Good evening, children, you have a beautiful dog. What breed is he? I've never seen a dog like him before! Does he like doughnuts?

- He loves them.

- It's a good thing that Bill and I have prepared two bags: one with chocolates and the other with coconut fritters. Are you happy?

- Oh, yes, ma'am, and thank you. Goodbye, see you next year.

- It's your turn, Rino.

- Knock... knock... knock... knock... Treat or Trick?

- I'll give you "Treat *or* Trick", *you* bastard dog! I'll give you a good kick in the butt. And you, you little punks, you bad seed! Disturbing honest people at such a late hour! I'll report you to the police.

- Rino, the mustard is going up my nose. I'm going to shut his mouth. Look out! Look out! Look out! I stare into his eyes, wiggling my moustache three times. One, two, three.......

The old man stops with his mouth wide open.

- But... but... but... what did your dog do to her?

- Don't be afraid Mike, he'll stay like a statue for half an hour, then he'll wake up and not remember a thing.

- I saw the same thing on TV. I get it, you're Martians.

- No, I'm Italian and I live in Switzerland with my family. Osiris is Egyptian and of royal blood. Certain powers were passed down to him by his grandmother. We're here to celebrate Halloween.

- Ah! I got it. I got it. Rino, you go on with the houses on the right side of the street and I'll go on with the houses on the left. We'll meet in an hour at the crossroads...

- Phew! We combed the whole neighborhood. What a great harvest!

- Thanks, Mike. It's because of your help.

- Sit down on the lawn and divide the loot equally, I'll just lift my paws on this flower bed.

- I'll let you do Rino, I'm not good at math.

- 10 bars of chocolate, 24 doughnuts, 6 candy cones... That's not bad. Here's your cut, Mike.

- Thank you, Rino, I'm leaving you my friends, my parents are waiting for me. Come and visit me, I live at number 3658 in the house painted red, the third street on the left.

- Yeah, yeah, bye Mike, see you soon.

- Rino, the time is coming up, let's put the sheet back in its place and let's get back on the way home. We have to get to Geneva before your parents wake up. Let's fly over the city of lights in a hurry. It's a fairy tale show.

- Yeah, they look like thousands of Christmas trees!

- I hear nine bells ringing in St. Patrick's Cathedral. It's already three o'clock in the morning in Geneva. Quickly, let's go... This vast expanse is Alaska, the kingdom of the Nordic dogs, and to our right, the sea! These blocks of ice that emerge are icebergs.

- Yes, my teacher told us about it. Sometimes they sink ships.

- One... two... three... We've arrived safely.

- Last night you broke all speed records.

- The Geneva sky is tinged with pink. Perhaps it will snow!

- I've never seen snow in Sicily. If it snowed, I could throw balls and make a snowman instead of going to school. You're lucky Osiris, you sleep, eat and laze all day long.

- Selfish boy, don't forget that I often spend my nights carrying you on my back, and you're not a lightweight. On the other hand, I think, prepare our travels, and when you brood, I console you.

- Excuse me, my dear Osiris, I thank you for all your devotion. Here's our building, the wind didn't blow out the window.

- Let's go in quietly, one... ...two...

- Ouch! Ouch! I hit my toe on my truck.

- Damn it! Your mother woke up.

- Rinoooo... Rinoooo! What's going on? What's going on? Are you sick? I'll be right over.

- Rino, quickly close your eyes and walk with outstretched arms! I lie at the foot of the bed. Come what may!

- Oh my God!... my little Rino! He's standing on the dresser. He has become a sleepwalker. What a misfortune! I have a son who sleepwalks!

Rino, arms outstretched, eyes fixed, walks to his bed and stretches out on the blanket. His relieved mother closes the window and goes back to her room. Rino gets up, hides the loot in his satchel and stows it under his bed. Then we fall asleep as one.

At noon, we were still sound asleep. Worried, Rino's mother made a doctor's appointment the same day. After a serious examination, the paediatrician diagnosed a severe fatigue and a lack of vitamins.

- He needs rest, padlock the window of his room! Says the doctor. An accident is always possible during sleepwalking attacks.

- Osiris, what a catastrophe! We won't be able to travel anymore.

- Calm down, my friend. Grandma Isis taught me how to open a padlock without a key. With my sharp lugs, no lock can resist me. There's nothing to stop us from visiting the whole universe. Grandma Isis always said that travel is what youth is all about.

That night, Rino dreamt that he went back to his Nonna and drank some good, frothy goat's milk. When he woke up, he said to me.

- Osiris, I'm feeling blue. I'd like to see Sicily again.

- Chase away your gloomy thoughts, we'll go when the almond trees are in bloom.

Reassured, he went to school without moaning.

7. HOLLAND

- Melancholy is painted on your face my friend, are you in pain?

- I'm thinking of my sunny Sicily.

- You'll see her again soon; tonight, I set my sights on Holland. Get ready, don't forget your scarf and mittens!

- Aye, aye, sir!

- We are lucky, the moon pours out a silvery light and the wind pushes us in the right direction. Have you ever heard of this country?

- No, I'm waiting for you to explain.

- Holland is a country where the sea is higher than the land.

- We're going to drown; we should have brought a lifebuoy.

- No, the Dutch are brave and far-sighted. They have been fighting violent attacks from the sea for centuries. They mastered the waters and protected themselves from floods by building dykes, dams, locks and mechanical pumps. They have created polders by draining the submerged land and they enrich the country by cultivating them.

- It's interesting, I'm looking forward to seeing the sea.

- Beneath our feet lie vast fields dotted with ponds where ducks frolic. I see two of them pointing towards the clouds.

- Stop, Osiris! Ouch, ouch, ouch! I can't feel my head.

- Excuse me, Rino, I was distracted, I didn't see that windmill. You hit your forehead against a wing. I'll land by that river and I'll fix you up...

- Show me your forehead... You have a huge bump! Put this stone on it! With the cold, the bump will fade away. It's a remedy from grandmother Isis, she was ingenious. From now on we'll be more careful because we'll often encounter windmills. Not long ago, they were used to pump water. Today the machines have taken their place. Do you feel better, my friend?

- Yes, thank you, Osiris.

- Get in the saddle and let's hit the road!

- The sea! The sea!

- Yes, we are near the port of Rotterdam. All these ships are moored under their national flags.

- I see barges and scows unloading, but what are they doing on the wharf?

- They're giant cranes.

- Cranes? Aren't they birds?

- Yes, but these are lifting devices; Rotterdam is Europe's largest port and its traffic is very important. This public garden invites us to stop. Let's sit by those statues!

- Are they teddy bears?

- Yes, Bronze Bears! You can pet them; their noses have already been polished by thousands of childish palms.

- Are you rested?

- Yes, my dear guide.

- Let's wander around this neighborhood. Look in that window: parrots!

- Oh, they're chained to their perch!

- And they get all self-conscious and say "ke ke ke ke ke ke ke ke ke " like a windbag.

- What do they mean?

- Set us free, "ke ke ke ke ke".

- I want to break the glass so they can fly away.

- Get that idea out of your head and get on that bike. I'll take this one.

- Osiris, I've never been on a bicycle!

- Take your courage in both hands and try. Every good, self-respecting Dutch citizen drives around in this vehicle. Grab the handlebars, put your left foot on the pedal and your butt on the saddle! Grab the other pedal with your right foot and pedal, pedal, pedal! Bravo, the wheels are turning...

Patatras! There's Rino on the floor!

- Osirisssss! My ankle hurts.

- Get up! Get up!

- I, I, I, I can't, my scarf got wound up in the stacks... Ow, ow, ow, ow!

- Stop complaining, I'm coming...

- You haven't broken anything, only a little bruise on your thigh! I put everything back in order. Get up and do it again!... Bravo, bravo, it's perfect! You're a champion cyclist!... Rino, Rino, stop! You'll fall into the sea...

- Help Osiris, I can't stop!

- Hit the brakes!

- I don't know how to brake.

- Press the lever under the handlebars!

Phew, he maneuvered in time!

- You scared the hell out of me! I'm a mediocre driving instructor. Let's lean our vehicles against that wall, get back to our usual means of transport and drive all the way to Amsterdam. Can you hear the children singing?

Amsterdam the big city
is built on stilts
If one day she falls down
Who will pay the bill?

- Is it really built on stilts?

- Yes, the city is built on more than 13,000 stilts and is criss-crossed by numerous canals. Let's walk along the Amstel canal. It is the most important and it leads us to the Dam square.

- What animation! It's a disturbing sight.

- Pull yourself together. In front of us stands the royal palace, where the queen presents herself to greet her subjects.

- A queen in the flesh?

- Of course, look, up there on the balcony, that lady dressed in moon-colored silk and adorned with a glittering tiara, it's her! That's Her Majesty the Queen with the Prince.

- How beautiful she is! Are the crown diamonds real?

- Yes, she carries a fortune on her head! Don't forget that the city is a diamond center! The people of Amsterdam cut and polish fine and precious stones. The last time I visited the city, I went to the diamond district. I went into a jeweler's shop to ask about the price of a pink diamond. I wanted to buy it as a gift for my mother. No sooner had I opened the door than I was chased away with an umbrella. I don't regret anything, that day I had forgotten to take some florins with me.

- Let's get away from this crowd and stroll through the Indonesian restaurant district.

- Hmm, what a smell comes out of those pots! It tickles my nostrils.

- Wait for me on this bench, I see on a table a leftover rice and chicken curry. It's been so long since I've eaten any! The envy devours me. I'm going to lick the plate and come back...

- The waiter is a rude man! No sooner had I finished gnawing the chicken leg than he chased me with a white napkin. It was good! I'm licking my chops. Are you hungry, my friend?

- Yeah, my stomach's growling.

- Take from the pouch under my collar a twenty-guilder bill and order from this travelling merchant some herring saur and a grilled eel. Also buy a portion of mussels. You'll offer me some, I'm fond of them.

- I'm enjoying it! Use mussels!

- They are fresh and well-seasoned. Are you full?

- Yes, my stomach is full.

- So now let's go and visit the house of the painter Rembrandt.

- I like to draw and paint; Mrs. Merle tells me I'm good at it.

- Persevere, you may become famous. Artists abound in this country. Tonight, we have little time to visit museums. Next time I'll introduce you to the painters Vermeer, Bruegel, Van Gogh and many others.

- We'll be back for St. Nicholas' Day. It is celebrated on December 6th. Mark that date in your diary. On that day, you will meet a monk dressed in a red tassel and with a face decorated with a flowery white beard. He will be accompanied by Peter the Cursed. Peter is a demon. In the past, to atone for his sins, he used to walk on the rooftops and drop toys and sweets down the chimneys. He got tired of his solitary walk and became a prisoner of St. Nicholas. Today, they both distribute rewards to the wise children.

- Osiris, look! A piano is pulled out of the window with a rope.

- Hi, hi, hi, hi! You're witnessing a move. The Dutch do it through the windows, because the stairs in the houses are too narrow. They can't get the furniture up and down.

- My word! They didn't tighten the rope enough! It will untie itself and let go of the piano.

- What music we're going to hear!

Bmmmmmmmmmmmmm!

- I know that young people in Amsterdam enjoy pop music and jazz, but not this cacophony.

- The piano is smashed!

- I feel sorry for the movers. We'll soap their heads... The clouds are gathering, let's get to Harlem before it rains. I want to show you a statue of a child.

- Why did he deserve this honor?

- It is said that he saved the country from a flood by plugging a crack in a dyke with his finger. His act was considered heroic...

- The clouds dissipate, Madam Moon reappears! Where are we now? I'm slowing down, you, get your flashlight out of your pants pocket!

- Here it is, I'm lighting up. I see big red, yellow and blue spots on the ground.

- These are fields of flowers, hold on! I'm landing in a tulip field.

- Osiris, so many flowers and what a perfume!

- Yes, daffodils and hyacinths scent the air. Behind us is a bed of daffodils.

- The smell of these flowers intoxicates me. My head is spinning.

- Come back down to earth and relax in rose heaven.

- The scent of roses makes me gray. Ow, ow, ow, my nose!

- What's happening to him?

- I stuffed him into a red rose and a wasp stung me.

- You disturbed her, she was drinking the flower juice. Indeed you look like a clown. I dig up a tulip onion and rub your nose. A remedy recommended by my Aunt Nephthys.

Zoom in... zoom... zoommmmmmmmmmmm...

- What's that strange snore?

- These are the race cars of the Zandvoort circuit. If the Gods turn me into a man one day, my greatest desire would be to compete in the Dutch Grand Prix...

- The sea, the sea! A fairy tale in the color of Argentina!

- This is the North Sea. Wink to the right, spy on the deer park and to the left look at the bird garden... Master Fox, Isengrin the Wolf and Grimpert the Badger are on the lookout and whet their appetites. Ah, what a nice bite they would make with the inhabitants of these aviaries!

- Careful, Osiris, you're gassing on the lighthouse.

- Thank you, Rino, his brilliance blinds me, he's signalling the airport. This aerodrome notes an altitude of less than four meters below sea level. Let's stop and walk on the dike. We have an impressive sight and view. On one side, the Ijsel lake undulates and in front of it the enemy sea stirs and opens its arms to infinity. A gull spreads its wings and rises in the clouds; let's imitate it!

- What about the statue of the little boy?

- That'll have to be another time. Hold yourself close to my body, you're cold, my hair will warm you up. I'm speeding up the pace... fifteen... ten.... five... We're arriving safely and the window is still open.

- What an exciting hike! I'm becoming a man of great knowledge, but I have goose bumps.

- Put your clothes on the radiator and bury yourself under the quilt!

That night, Rino dreamt he was flying on the back of a duck. They landed on the moon and then Rino woke up on the bedside rug. His mother ran up and took him in her arms. Rino had a small bump on his forehead and a bruised nose. She made him ice water compresses and rubbed an ointment on his nose. An hour later, he had lunch and went to school refreshed.

8. ALASKA

Sitting in the kitchen waiting for Rino, I'm enjoying some delicious ravioli. His mother cooks them so well that every time I let myself be tempted. I should avoid this food because it's not good for my figure. I greedily lick the plate when Rino arrives.

- Hello Osiris, I attended a wonderful puppet show, and do you know who I met along the way?

- Who's there? Say quickly Rino!

- A wolf! A young man had him on a leash

- A wolf? That surprises me. It must have been a Nordic dog. There's one in the neighborhood. Describe it to me.

- Well, he was tall, very tall, pearl gray color, pointed snout with a white mask around the brown and oval eyes. His ears stood up on his head like those of a wolf and his tail curled up like a trumpet.

- I know her as Inouk, a female *malamute,* a very old breed from Alaska. A *malamute* dog weighs about forty kilos and can pull a load of eight to nine hundred kilos. Eskimos use them to pull their sleds.

- Are they bad?

- No, they're gentle, affectionate dogs. They are very rare in Europe.

- When I met her, she put her paws on my shoulders, I thought she wanted to bite me. But no, it was to lick my face.

- By the way, what day is it?

- Wednesday, why are you asking me this question?

- Do you have a written test tomorrow?

- No. No, no, no, no, no, no, no.

- So tonight, I'll take you to Alaska, we'll watch a Nordic dog race.

- At nightfall, I whisper in my friend's ear.

- Dress warmly, the temperature in northern Alaska drops to minus ten and sometimes as low as minus twenty degrees in March. Button up the coat that your mother had the good idea to knit for me! When we get there, I'll press down on the green stone of my collar, it will radiate a gentle warmth that will keep my body from getting cold. The first time I went to Alaska with Grandma Isis, I almost died. All my limbs were stiff and my muzzle was purple. I had left my necklace by the tomb of the Pharaoh. Grandma Isis warmed me with her breath. We had gone to search for gold. She found a nugget in a riverbed that weighed five kilos. She danced with joy... Have you put on your long underwear?

- Yes.

- You have grumbled enough and told your mother that they were old-fashioned; tonight, they will be useful to you.

- All right, Osiris, from now on I'll be more docile. I tie my shoes and I'm ready.

- One... two... three, on the way to Russia. In prehistoric times, Siberia and Alaska were connected, nowadays only a strait separates them.

- Is it cold all over the country?

- No, the center has a temperate climate. Right now, we're over the Bering Strait, St. Lawrence Island, and this is Alaska.

- And this mountain, is it the Himalayas?

- No, but Mount McKinley. When I think of Mrs. Merle certifying you as the class genius, I shudder to think of the other students. The area around that mountain is protected, it's a nature reserve. It's forbidden to hunt or pick flowers.

- Osiris! Osiris! A rainbow!

- We are in the presence of the aurora borealis. Electrified particles from the sun collide with the earth's atmosphere and produce this luminous arc from which jets of light are emitted into space.

- What a great show!

- Especially with the dark sky. We're over the Arctic. In winter, the day is short and not very bright; in summer, the sun sometimes shines twenty-four hours a day. It's the midnight sun... Now we are approaching the town of North Pole, which means "the North Pole". That's where Santa Claus lives. Thousands of little Americans write to him every year.

- I'd like to go, do me a favor, Osiris!

- All right, I'm going to land near that hut... Damn it, damn it! I tripped over a stump of dead wood.

- Are you in pain, Osiris?

- No, the snow cushioned the shock... Don't expect to meet Santa Claus, he's just a legend!

- I'm not a baby anymore.

Suddenly, a thunderous voice rang out:

- Who says there's no Santa Claus?

- In our bewilderment, we search for the source of this voice. A tall man with a white beard, sitting on a tree trunk with his hands on his hips is watching us.

- Hello sir, who are you?

- I'm Santa Claus, if you don't like it! Are you surprised? I'm no stranger than a flying dog. I admired your surprising landing. I was scanning the horizon with my binoculars. What are you looking for?

- We want to see the finish of the Nordic dog race.

- Where did you come from?

- We are from Switzerland; my name is Rino and my dog Osiris. We've come for the harness race.

- My buck Diak went to glean the latest news.

A deer with a red nose like a tomato lies gracefully in front of us and screams:

- Santa Claus! Santa Claus! The first ones are coming and I think Oukiok's carriage is in the lead.

- Diok, meet Rino and Osiris, two foreigners who come to welcome the winners.

- Pleased to meet you; I am the red-nosed deer to serve you. I guide Santa Claus as he distributes gifts to all the children of the world.

Are we dreaming? Is it a mirage? I rub my eyes and Rino pinches his thigh.

No, because Santa says:

- Come visit my workshops, then I'll offer you a snack. Get in that cave!

Little dwarves dressed in rainbow-colored costumes are bustling around large steaming vats.

- These make barley sugars and lollipops; those in the second cave make wooden games... Are you convinced that I am Santa Claus?

- Yes, yes, Santa.

- Come and have a bite to eat!

He served us a delicious meal of smoked salmon, grilled crabs and ice cream flavored with blackberries.

- And now, let me introduce you to the six deer of my crew.

A female deer is staring at me insistently. I get confused and look away. Suddenly, she comes closer and slips into the hollow of my ear:

- You're the most elegant deer I've ever seen. I love your long silky ears and your almond-shaped eyes. Oh, my Prince Charming, come down from heaven, let's fly to the stars!

Rino bursts out laughing.

- She thinks you're a deer from another planet.

- To convince her of her mistake, I bark three times, signal my companion to jump on my back and we leave in the direction of the city of Nome.

- Osiris, how beautiful the city is under the illuminated snow! Do you hear the music?

- Yes, it's a holiday. All the houses are sporting the colors of their favorite carriages.

- A sled is sneaking through the trees!

- You've got good eyesight, let's land and mingle.

At last, the victorious crew appears. The crowd is shouting for joy.

They are seven *Malamutes* and the driver standing on his sled slaps his whip to encourage the animals. He is wrapped in a parka and his fur cap hides his face. He throws a "wow" sound, the Malamutes *stop*. The driver rushes on Oukiok and gives him a big kiss on his black nose. Then, he messes up his hair.

- It's a woman! Osiris! How pretty she is and what beautiful black hair!

- It's not the first time a woman has won! Let's go to the saloon to congratulate Oukiok, he's quenching his hunger.

- He must be starving, what's he eating?

- A leg of caribou.

- Good evening, Oukiok, we congratulate you on this great victory.

- Thank you, my friends, nice to meet you. And yes, luck was with us. We feared the *Siberian huskies*. These dogs often win races because they are lighter and faster than *Malamutes*.

- What nice boots you're wearing, Oukiok!

- They're *kamiks*, sealskin. They protect my paws from the ice needles... Please Rino, take my shoes off and remove the cotton from between my fingers... Thank you, my friend. Phew! It feels good to have my paws exposed.

- Is it your job to pull sleds?

- No, it's for my pleasure, in the everyday life, I work. I take part in races to keep in shape and not to weigh myself down. I eat too much; gluttony is my sweet sin.

- Dear Oukiok, tell me about the sleds and carriages, maybe I can build one for Osiris?

- No, no, I don't want it. Salukis are not draft dogs.

- Okay, okay, I didn't mean to offend you, I'm sorry!

- Dear friends, I'm exhausted, I'm leaving you and I'm going to lie on the straw.

- Good evening, Oukiok! Shoo, Rino, quickly, astride! Your eyelids are closing. I'm tired, I can't stand the low temperature... I'm speeding up, one... two... wake up... you're in your room, get undressed and good night!

That night, Rino dreamt that he was driving a sled with seven *salukis* up in the sky.

9. PRAGUE

It's the Christmas holidays; the street is brightened up by trees decorated with multicolored balls and light bulbs.

My boyfriend scans the sky hoping to find snowflakes flying around. Alone, the rain has been falling in large drops, without respite, for the past eight days. The wave at the soul, Rino tells me:

- Where could we go tonight, Osiris? I would so much like to see and touch the snow.

- Well, I have an idea, we'll go to Czechoslovakia. In winter, children make snowmen in town squares and skate on rivers. Bundle up, cover your head with your balaclava and put on your sheepskin boots!

- And you, how will you protect yourself from the cold?

- I'm wearing the red sweater with the white polka dots your mother knitted me... I hope my magic necklace will give off enough heat to keep my whiskers, tail and ears from turning to ice.

- What itinerary do you set up?

- We will fly over Switzerland to Zurich, then branch off to Austria and when the Bohemian mountains cut into the sky, we will be in Czechoslovakia. Saddle up for the big start!

- Osiris, the fog is thick, you can't see a drop.

- Yes, the airport's closed, the planes can't land. Thanks to my radar whiskers, there's no risk of collision. I don't think Prague, the capital, is foggy.

And here are our two companions on a journey to discover new horizons.

They hovered over high mountains, snow-covered forests and wild animals. It froze to the ground. Rino moved his legs tirelessly. Osiris told him:

- Stop it, you're confusing me!

- I can't help it, I'm cold and my teeth are rattling like castanets. No matter how hard I press the button on my collar, it doesn't give off much heat. My ears are starting to hurt. I can't feel my tail and we're losing altitude. I absolutely have to land.

- Yeah, it's safer.

- Where are we now? The snowflakes are blinding me.

- Above a snow-covered forest and a castle.

- I recognize it, it's Karlsejn Castle. We'll land and take refuge there, the walls are thick, they'll keep us out of the cold. It was built in the 14th century by the greatest king of Bohemia, Charles IV. This king hid in this fortress the jewels of the imperial crown.

- How did the castellans warm themselves in ancient times?

- In winter, they washed little and rarely changed their clothes. In the evening, they would gather around large fires and tell ghost stories.

- Ghosts? It doesn't exist, Osiris!

- What do you know, Rino?

- You can tell me anything you want; I don't believe in them and I'm not afraid of ghosts.

- All right, all right, let's get into the big tower!

- Oh! How beautiful!

Precious stones set in the walls and ceilings shone as long as we thought we were in broad daylight. Paintings of saints hung on the walls. Rino, amazed, contemplated these wonders. Suddenly he said to me:

- Do you hear that noise? What could it be?

- Probably rats or bats. They swarm in these old buildings.

- No, no, I hear chain noises.

- Osiris, I'm scared, let's hide behind this column!

Suddenly we saw a strange apparition, a being of light, transparent, in a nightgown, with chained feet. He was holding his head under his left arm. In his right hand, he was clutching a blood-red sword.

Rino was green with fear, and I must confess to you my friends that I myself wasn't very big on it. The returnee, for he was one, walked to the altar, and then turned round, pointing his sword in our direction, and in a sepulchral voice said to us:

- Who are you strangers and how dare you desecrate these sacred places?

- We... we... we're simple travelers lost in the snow and we shelter from the cold. And who are you, sir?

- Don't be afraid, I'm the Sûlcovac revenant. Know that we ghosts don't do any harm to living beings. Our worlds are separate. I am very unhappy because I have been punished for a big mistake and I am condemned to haunt the places of my crime for eternity.

- What did you do wrong?

- I was in charge of guarding the imperial treasure in the niche above the altar. One night I drank too much plum liquor and fell asleep. Surprised by the chief of guards, denounced to His Majesty King Charles, I was condemned to have my head cut off and metamorphosed on my way back. I'm to guard the treasure overnight until judgment day... How unhappy I am!

Holding his head in his lap, he sobbed his heart out. Gently, on tiptoes and paws, we moved away and left him to his grief.

- What a fright I've had, I won't be laughing when I'm told about ghosts.

- How's your tail and ears?

- They're slightly numb. Let's take shelter in that cave and light a good fire to warm ourselves.

- Fancy, I'm stacking twigs and logs. You, rub these two stones together. When the sparks come out, bring them close to the twigs, they'll ignite.

As soon as said, as soon as done!

What a great outbreak! It lights up the whole cave.

- Osiris, there are drawings on the walls. They look like deer and buffalo.

- Our ancestors, the men of the Stone Age, lived in the caves and drew their everyday deeds. Bring a twig close to the wall, you'll be able to see the details better. You see, there's a rhinoceros, there's a...

- Osiris?

- What is it, Rino?

- One of our ancestors must survive nearby. Look at my finger! It's covered in paint.

- Don't be ridiculous, Rino, it's been a long time since there were men in the Stone Age.

- What about the "Abominable Snowman"?

- You read too many comic books.

- Grr... grr... jrr... jrr... gh... ugh... arrhumph!

- You have a funny voice Rino, do you have a cold?

- No, I'm not the one....

A strange small and rambunctious character, hidden behind a stalagmite was watching us. He presented us with a bestial physiognomy, a heavy and thick face, a receding chin and a low forehead. In his right hand he held an axe carved from stone. Rino, his eyes frozen with fear jumped on my back and, invigorated by the fire, I could finally fly away. The bewildered little man watched us leave.

- That was a close call, Osiris!

- Yes, deep in these isolated caves, some beings have managed to survive and reproduce for millennia. Perhaps it was an "abominable snowman"? I think we'd better get back to our penates... Let's fly over the Tatra Mountains and do some low flying, hopefully we'll see some animals.

- Osiris, Osiris... a family of wolves! They're huddled behind a tree. I recognize your cousin from the zoo in Vincennes, the one with a gash in his left ear.

- That's him, let's go down and say hello!... Oops, oops, oops cousin, do you recognize us?

- What a surprise! These are our visitors from Geneva. Welcome, in the language of the country, we say: "vitati *koho*". Let me introduce you to my wife Dushka and my two offspring Ishka and Sacha.

- We are happy to see you again. These little ones have grown up so much!

- Isn't that right? They're eight months old. In four months, they'll be hunting alone.

- How did you come to Czechoslovakia?

- France is not a safe country for us. There are too many hunters there and they decimate all the game. We had nothing left to eat. We had to fall back on sheep. We fled the country when we heard that the peasants were organizing beatings to kill the big wild dogs that were attacking their herds. We travelled through Belgium, Germany and finally settled in this country where we met our brothers, the wolves. Here they don't chase us too much. Of course, it was not easy to study Czech. It is a very difficult language.

- We're delighted to hear from you. We've had some terrible adventures too. Alas, the dawn is approaching, we must not linger any longer. We'll be back, goodbye and good luck, dear cousins!

- *Stâstnou cestu, Dobrou noc*! means good journey and good night.

- *Dobrou noc*!

- Osiris, we haven't visited the capital Prague.

- It's only a rain check, let's go home quickly!

- I'm tired, I have a headache, and my ears are ringing, I feel feverish. Perhaps I've caught a cold?

Rino had a restless sleep. He woke up with a red face and a high temperature. His mother called the doctor who diagnosed measles and forced him to stay in bed. When he was cured, the holidays were over. He went back to school too soon and contracted bronchitis. I kept him awake and thought it would be safer to wait until spring to start our travels again.

Finally, the buds burst and the trees became covered with leaves. I was titillated by the thought of our future hikes. I said to Rino:

- You've recovered, my friend. The new season invites us to travel.

- Oh yes, Osiris, inactivity weighs on me and I am thirsty for knowledge. What are your future plans?

- I have different ideas, let's sleep, at night let's take advice!

10. THE PHILIPPINES

The next day, Rino came home from school excited.

- Osiris, Osiris!

- What is it, Rino? Tonight, you're very agitated. What's the matter, Rino?

- I'm not the only foreigner in my class anymore!

- Is that right? Has a fellow countryman by any chance joined you?

- No, it's a boy from the Fili Islands... Fili... Damn, I can't remember the name. He speaks English, Spanish and one other language.

- Your comrade must be a Filipino and probably speaks *Tagalog*.

- Yes, that's right, you know everything, Osiris!

- Have you ever been to this country?

- Oh, it's been a long time. I went there with Grandma Isis. She absolutely wanted to go to the Philippines to see the cockfights which were very frequent at that time. She gambled and won a small fortune and a rooster named Miguel. Ah, I will remember Miguel! He had taken up residence in the Pyrenos pyramid. You know that pharaohs were always buried with their personal belongings, and food for their journey to the afterlife. Miguel discovered wheat in a jar and found nothing better than to devour it all. Pharaoh Montankhatou was furious!

- What happened to Miguel?

- He perished in the pyramid; I regret it, because he was a good companion, and with age he had grown mellow. Grandma Isis and I also went to the horse races in Manila. Filipinos love to play; do you know that?

- Yes, Enrique already taught me how to play dice. And I introduced him to a card game. We played battle; he really enjoyed it. But where are the Philippine Islands, is that in India?

- No, they're in Asia, in the Pacific Ocean near China. It's an archipelago.

- What is an archipelago, Osiris?

- It's a set of islands arranged in groups. There are more than three thousand of them, all mountainous and volcanic, only two thirds are inhabited. One of the largest is Luzon, where the most famous city is Manila. Its climate is tropical.

- Why does Enrique speak Spanish?

- Well, because of the history of the Philippines. I'll give you a brief overview. The first known inhabitants were Malays who came by boat from the nearby islands. In the 16th century, they were colonized by the Spaniards. In 1896, tired of the foreigners' yoke, the Filipinos revolted and called the Americans for help. This war lasted two years. Then the Americans, in turn, took over the territory. The Filipinos had several successive occupations. In 1946, Allah be praised, they regained their freedom.

- It is not fair that some countries invade the weakest nations!

- Of course, and it's usually to appropriate their wealth.

- Osiris, tell me, why don't we go to the Philippines tonight?

- That's good; I didn't have an itinerary planned. We'll fly out at nightfall.

- An hour after dinner, we were on our way,

- Oh Osiris, so many stars in the sky!

- Yes, in the tropics you can distinguish them much better than in Europe... We fly over Indonesia... Ah, here's Malaysia... over there are the Philippine islands.

- They're shaped like a crescent moon!

- That's right; aren't you too hot, Rino?

- Yes, and I'm a heavy headed man.

- The wind's picking up. I'm nervous, it's a bad omen.

- What is it, Osiris?

- Oh, nothing yet. Don't worry about it. We're coming up over Manila and we'll have the bay all lit up.

- It's beautiful!

- Here stands the famous Manilla Hotel, and further on, the port with the walled part of the old town within the city walls. That snake that runs through the city is the Pasig River. Next to it stands Fort Santiago.

- I think the capital is Manila.

- Make no mistake, the capital is called Quezon City, after the first president. It was built on the outskirts, where it's quieter to run the country. We're going to land in the country. There you'll see how Filipino peasants live in villages called *barrio*. Look, look, look, look!

- What funny little houses! I've never seen one like this, they stand on wooden stakes.

- We call these houses *nipa*. The walls and roofs are made of palm leaves on a bamboo frame. They are built on stilts to keep them dry during the rainy season. Underneath, the chickens and little black pigs live. The peasants also store their tools there. These houses are weatherproof for two or three years. When they can no longer stand upright, new ones are built. Well, let's rest in this tobacco field. The country is famous for its cigars. Grandma Isis brought my father two boxes of them. I smoked half a cigar in secret when I was very young. These cigars are very strong! For two days, I was sick as a dog, it's true to say!

- Osiris, I'm afraid! Look what's coming towards us. Let's hide quickly!

- What's that?

- A huge buffalo with huge curved horns is heading our way. My legs are wobbly.

- Ah, ah, ah! It's just a harmless *Carabao* coming to meet us. A what?

- A *carabao is* the most common draught animal used by peasants, the *taos,* as they are called here. He works with his master in the rice fields. He is peaceful, the little children climb on his back and wash him at the river.

- You reassure me, Osiris. I was scared to death; he doesn't look like a Swiss cow. But you look very funny, Osiris, I've never seen you in such a state.

- The wind is picking up, it's starting to blow very hard. I understand my nervousness, a typhoon is approaching. Let's not stay out in the open, we risk being blown away like straw fetuses. Jump on my back, let's reach the mountain and take refuge inside the forest...

- While waiting for it to pass, let's breathe in the smell of the fir trees and beeches! It's like being on a Swiss mountain, don't you think?

- Yes, but explain to me what a typhoon is.

- It is a violent storm that frequently rages in the South Seas. It causes terrible devastation and flooding. This one is light, we're only going to wipe its tail.

- Was he the reason you were so nervous? I didn't feel anything.

- Animals are closer to nature than humans. As soon as a natural phenomenon occurs, we perceive it. Our senses are more developed than yours. Have you noticed that a few hours before a storm breaks out, all the birds stop singing?

- Yes, and my cousin's poodle is hiding under his bed long before the storm hits.

- Brrr... it's dark as an oven; lucky my eyes sparkle.

- Osiris, isn't it time for dinner? I'm so hungry!

- Let's pick some fruit, these are excellent. Take one.

- It gives off a stench! Just like poo!

- Yes, but the pulp is delicious, this fruit is a dourian.

- Well, you can eat it, the smell makes me sick.

- As you like; taste the bananas, they are small and very sweet. Here, have one.

- Um... you're right, they are succulent. Osiris, stop eating! I feel like we're being watched.

- Maybe it's the *Negritos*.

- The what?

- The *Negritos*. They are pygmies, men with coffee-coloured complexion and frizzy hair, they are small, as petite as you are. They live in the forest. They're shy, but become ferocious if disturbed. They hunt with poisoned arrows. Come on, if they're watching us, you'd better show us. Let's go to that clearing.

We were soon surrounded by a cloud of *Negritos*, curious to see a white man and a dog. I said a few words to Rino, and they retreated as one man. Of course, they had never heard of a dog, and they thought we were deities brought by the typhoon.

We were taken to a campfire where we were made to sit on the ground. Then we were offered appetizing pieces of grilled meat, tasty mangos and juicy papayas.

Rino while chewing a piece of meat says to me:

- This meat is tender and exquisite, is it chicken?

- No, right now you're tasting parrot. On these leaves, they offer you monkey meat flavored with herbs.

- Monkey! If I didn't have a pit in my stomach, I wouldn't be touching it.

- We're lucky they're not cannibals.

- If you keep this up, you're going to scare me. But what do they want?

- Look, they're beckoning me to follow them to that canopy of foliage... Oh, there's a *Negrito* woman under it.

- Ah, ah, ah, ah, what the hell am I doing! My dear Rino, congratulations!

- Congratulations and why?

- They do you a great honor, the chief offers you his daughter in marriage.

- Get married? No, no, I don't want to, I'm still a little boy, save me Osiris, I want to go back to my mother!

Before I could even act, the *Negritos* had taken Rino to his bride. In order to counter any attempt by the bridegroom to escape, two witnesses...

stood behind him with their bows outstretched.

Rino was shaking like a leaf, I had to do something.......

First sniff... second sniff... third sniff... and here I am in the air, moving gracefully over their heads. Taking advantage of this moment of surprise and panic, I land near Rino, who jumps swiftly on my back. We take off, leaving the flabbergasted *Negritos* behind. The wind had died down, the typhoon had gone away. As we flew over Manila, we saw overturned garbage cans, uprooted trees and many *nipa* houses burned down.

- Say, Osiris! Can't we do anything to stop a typhoon?

- No, nature is stronger than man. With satellites we can detect them and evacuate the population of the cities in its path in time.

- Thank you, Osiris, as I travel, I become a scientist. I surprise my teacher. The other day when I was answering her questions, she was looking at me with eyes as big as marbles. She summoned mom and whispered to her "your son is a little genius; he needs to be examined by a ps... si... psi... "

- A psychologist?

- Yes, a school psychologist; maybe he'll find out I'm smart! Now Mrs. Merle is nicer and more considerate.

- She makes me sit next to her and tells me not to get too tired.

- Well, in the meantime, here we are. Let's get some rest, geniuses need a lot of sleep. They need to recharge their batteries.

That night, Rino dreamt that he was riding on the back of a *carabao* and a monkey was pulling his hair.

11. FIRE

Tonight, I don't know what's going on. No matter how many sheep I count and recount in the sky, I can't sleep a wink. I'm angry and I can't breathe. It seems to me that there's a scorching smell in the room. But Rino's mother isn't in the kitchen anymore, she's asleep. I'm worried, so I'm going to call my friend.

- Rinoooo.... Rinooooooo... Wake up! Wake up!

He's sound asleep. I'm going to tickle the soles of his feet.......

He's still not waking up! I nibbled his ear... Nothing to do, he sleeps like a log. Then I pull his hair.

- Ouch! Ouch! Oh là là, my head! Where am I, Osiris? It's so hot! I dreamt I was climbing Mount Etna. Multicolored flames were gushing out of the crater and burning lava was flowing down the rocks. Sweat was running down my body and...

- You can tell me the rest of your dream some other time. I'm not on the edge of a crater, but I'm suffocating. Turn the switch quickly

- so that we can see clearly... Oh, the room is smoky! My eyes sting, open the window! I'll bark and you call your parents. Wow! Wow ... arooooo ... Puahuahuah!

- Daddy, Mummy! Help me!

- What a din in Rino's room, do you hear Maria? And I have to get up at five o'clock and they don't let me sleep! Maria, shut them up!

- Daddy, Mommy, help! Wake up! Wake up! We are smoked.

- Maria, what does Rino say?

- Jump out of bed and turn on the light, he's talking about smoke.

- Good heavens, it's true! It's no longer a room, it's a smokehouse. Let's not panic. I'll put on my trousers and you, Maria, put on your dressing gown. Hurry up and wrap Pietro in a blanket! I'm going to see where this smoke is coming from.

- Oh, but she's coming up from the cellar! Quick, Maria, close the door, the house is burning!

- I'll call the fire department and I'll wake up all the tenants. Go with the little one on the balcony! Rinooooo! Rino, stay in your room!

- Yes, yes, daddy... Osiris, I'm trembling with fear.

- Calm down, Rino! Fire, police and ambulance cars are coming. I hear the alarm siren.

Pim pam, pim pam, pim pam, pim pam....

- Rino, draw the curtain! Look, look, look, look! All the lights come on and the windows open. The onlookers are running in from all sides. The officers stretch out ropes to keep the crowd away. The fire department is setting up the ladders against our building. They roll out the water hoses. Allah be praised! They work, water gushes out.

- Somebody help me! Come and get me or I'll throw myself off the balcony!

- Do you hear Rino? That's Mrs. Miltonne's voice.

- Yes Osiris, and I see Marianne Beausoleil on her balcony. She has a beautiful red kimono. A fireman takes her in his arms... Tell me,

- Osiris, how are we going to deal with Mrs. Miltonne? She's so fat! But are we forgotten? I'm anxious. Save me, Osiris!

- You're right, we have to do something. The floor is hot, I don't know where to put my paws. The flames are starting to invade the room. Ow! Ow! Ow! I burned my left ear. If we wait for the rescuers, I'll lose all my strength. Get on my back, I'll try to use my right ear. Are you ready? One, two, three come what may! Let's jump out the window!

The crowd gathered around the building, astonished, followed Rino and the dog. A child screamed:

- Oh look, a dog with a child on its back! It looks like it's flying.

- But it's true! The dog flies! Look, look, it's landing!

- Back, everybody, get back! You all right, boy?

- Yes, Officer, but I think my dog has a broken leg.

- We'll take care of it, come with me.

- No, no, I don't want to leave my dog... sniff, sniff... I want my parents.

- Don't cry, little one. That lady holding a boy in her arms, isn't that your mother?

- Yes, Mama! Mama! I'm in here. Where's daddy?

- Don't worry, little one! Your father is a brave man. Just like the captain of a ship, he wanted to take out the last one. We are saved, but what a disaster! So many flames! Everything is burning! We lost everything.

- Don't cry mummy, thanks to Osiris, we are safe and sound.

- This way, folks, this way. Get in this car... come on, ladies and gentlemen, come on, we'll take you to a hotel. You're going to eat and rest.

- Thank you, officer. Madame Beausoleil, you go first.

- Please, Mrs. Salvatore, sit down with your children! Ah, you're here too, Osiris!

- Do you know, dear Madame Beausoleil, he's the one who gave the alarm.

- Really? How strange! This is the second time he's saved my life.

The humans slept several nights at the Hotel de la Paix. As for me, I was treated in a clinic. A veterinarian immobilized my leg with splints. Now it's healed and I can run again. My left ear with third degree burns is atrophied. I can hear, I can talk, but I can't fly anymore!!!!

The local press reported that the fire was set by an arsonist... There was also talk of the dog Saluki, thanks to whom all the tenants were saved. I was the hero of the day.

Rino went back to school and had his hands full answering all the questions his classmates asked him. Now we are living in a new, well-furnished apartment that is bigger than the old one.

Joy has returned to the family as Rino's mother is expecting a happy event. Rino hopes that his mother will give birth to a little sister.

In the evening we both chat and reminisce about our travels. Rino takes notes in a notebook. He's thinking about writing a book. I'm not sad that I don't fly because I believe in the power of the gods and I know that grandmother Isis watches over me and tries the impossible to help me regain my faculties. I help Rino as best I can with his homework while I wait for the miracle.

About the Author

Fanny Mouchet (1923-2011) is the mother of the filmmaker Louis Mouchet and the wife of the poet Charles Mouchet (1920-1979), for whom she illustrated most of his publications.

In addition to an apprenticeship as a seamstress, she attended evening classes at the Academy of Fine Arts from which she graduated.

She then became a teacher of young children.

The last part of her life was devoted to the Geneva Writers' Society of which she was an essential pillar.